D1300838

Bibliographical Monograph No. 1

Suppressed Commentaries

on

The Wiseian Forgeries

Addendum to an Enquiry

BY WILLIAM B. TODD

Humanities Research Center
THE UNIVERSITY OF TEXAS AT AUSTIN

To John Carter and Graham Pollard
Whose Original Enquiry Will Lead to Endless
Addenda on The Work of T. J. Wise

Foreword

This monograph represents the first in a series resting primarily on the bibliographical resources available at the University of Texas or on other aspects of manuscript and book production which may constitute the discourse of visiting lecturers. Expected shortly is another essay, by Professors Kendall and Bratcher, on T. J. Wise's shameful dealings in 1910–1914 with the Boston Bibliophile Society. Also being readied for the press is *The Permanence of Gutenberg*, a paper given here in 1968 by Frederick R. Goff, President of the Bibliographical Society of America, and first speaker in the Lew David Feldman Lectureship Program. The next speaker, this year, will be Sir Frank Francis, retired Director and Principal Librarian of the British Museum.

It is hoped that the recital of things come, and to come, will merit the attention of bibliophiles everywhere and that this series will find a place where scholars may ever consult its varied contents.

WILLIAM B. TODD
GENERAL EDITOR

The University of Texas at Austin
13 May 1969

Wiseian Forgeries

CORRESPONDENCE recently acquired by The University of Texas reveals that, in 1934, no fewer than four different campaigns were undertaken by American nationals for or against the cause of T. J. Wise. Generally the intent of these communications, like others posted to English journals, was to elicit from Wise an adequate accounting of some 54 nineteenth-century pamphlets, all denounced in the Carter-Pollard *Enquiry*[1] as forgeries (29), suspect of forgeries (20), or piratical (5), and all further shown to be editions which Wise had handled and promoted.

Among the several American skirmishes the first two were directed by Charles F. Heartman,[2] bibliophile, consultant, appraiser, auctioneer, and editor of the *American Book Collector*. The other two were at the instigation of Gabriel Wells, bookseller, friend and, indeed, general confidant of all the more eminent collectors. Since both men operated independently, and often with opposite intent, their accounts are best considered apart, and sequentially of the order in which each begins.

1. Heartman and Wise

Before the *Enquiry* appeared Heartman started two files. The first was to contain relevant newspaper clippings and, later, reviews of the book. Item 1 here is a June 12th front-page dispatch from the New York *Herald-Tribune*. Titled "Literary 'Bomb' Brought in by Scribner Agent," this reports the arrival the day before of Charles Kingsley, head of the London branch of Scribner's, who was then proceeding, proofs in hand, to the New York office, designated as American publisher of the *Enquiry*. The proofs Kingsley refused to display, but a prospectus, listing the fifteen authors under examination, was freely distributed to assembled reporters and anxious bibliophiles.

Unfortunately, the interview was a day or two late for the publisher of the *American Book Collector*. Heartman had already sent to press the July issue and, in it, his own preliminary announcement. What he then reported came from correspondence published in the London papers and, in larger measure, from various gossip as to the number of authors involved. Altogether, Heartman mentions only six, nine short of those cited in the Kingsley handout.[3]

Several days later, when page proofs were returned, Heartman opened another file for the correspondence then initiated with Wise. His own letters and other material are, to our great advantage, preserved in typescript carbons. Letters from Wise, all but the last in the hand of his wife,[4] received even better treatment, for each is carefully mounted on a foolscap sheet. The file begins with a report conveying proofs of the commentary (pp. 200–201 in the journal) and, more to the point, raising the possibility of a statement. It ends, seven months later, with a plaintive note from Wise again rehearsing a defence which the Enquirers had earlier found unacceptable.

Interfiled with the correspondence are four other items of somewhat greater interest. Three are cablegrams, one from Heartman now urgently soliciting the statement, and two from Wise, the first expressing his outrage on reading the book, the second recalling the statement then prepared. Last and most significant is the statement itself, one long regarded as suppressed and destroyed,[5] but here recovered and exhibited in a form illustrating all its peculiarities. Readers interested only in this should now disregard what follows and turn immediately to the second entry for July 19.

June 14.   Heartman to Wise

Dear Mr. Wise:

In order that you may have as early as possible the preliminary statement of THE AMERICAN BOOK COLLECTOR in
reference to the affair now in the air I am enclosing herewith what we say in the next issue. You will get in due
course a week later a complete copy of the magazine.

I hope what I have written has not annoyed you too much.
Of course, I do these things in my own temperamental
way and must be permitted to continue. However, this does
not prevent me from saying that I am extremely friendly
to you and am fully convinced that you are not mixed up
whatsoever in this affair except perhaps as an innocent
victim.

The point I am trying to bring out is that I must go more
into details in this matter as soon as the book is out. The
number after the one which you will soon receive will be a
double number so there will be ample time to peruse the
evidence in the matter. You probably will receive a copy
yourself by that time. It is my great hopes [sic] that I can
persuade you to write an article for this double number of
my magazine giving your opinion of the whole affair and
the particular books under suspicion if you care to do so.
I will review the book and either let your article appear
ahead of mine or following mine. I do think you owe to
yourself the statement to the American public. We have
not such strict libel laws as in Great Britain in consequence
of which there is a lot of loose gossip going around much of
which is extremely damaging to you. Of course, a great
deal of it is done by irresponsible parties who could never
be taken to task but I do think THE AMERICAN BOOK COL-
LECTOR has a sufficient circulation to offset and counteract
any remarks the rabble may make. In the last month I have
persistently told everybody that I was fully convinced you
had nothing to do in this matter. I have done this in the

presence of others. Mr. Swann[6] will probably substantiate this statement of mine as will other dealers of prominence. Whenever the discussion came up and your name was mentioned I implied that you were so far above the matter that it was even unnecessary to mention this fact.

Very truly yours,
[s] Charles F. Heartman

June 25.   Wise to Heartman

This first response is on stationery of the Queen's Hotel, Hastings. Subsequent letters are posted from Wise's residence, 25 Heath Drive, Hampstead, London, N.W. 3.

Dear Mr. Heartman,

Thank you very much for your most interesting, & very kind letter of June 14th, together with the enclosed printed leaves, which reached me here this morning. It is evident that you know a great deal more about this coming book than I do. I have only heard vague & casual rumours from time to time, & have been able to ascertain hardly anything definite apart from the "Reading Sonnets." I am looking forward to reading the book upon its appearance a week or two hence; when I have done so I shall know exactly what it is all about. These two young men have not gone about their work in a very wise manner. They appear to have refrained altogether from consulting the very people who could have afforded them the best information. They have never been to Mr Forman,[7] or to me, or to first-class booksellers like Maggs Bros. I met Mr Ernest Maggs here about a week ago. He told me that Carter & Pollard "had tumbled into a big mare's nest." Carter, I have never seen,[8] but I understand he is employed in the book department at Scribners. Pollard is a very young man, apparently about 25 years of age.[9] I have only seen him once; that was last October[10] when he called one afternoon & asked me to tell him, where I had obtained my own copies of a list of books, most of which were small pamphlets which I bought in the ordinary manner for a few shillings each 40 or more years ago. He then told me about the Browning Sonnets. Of course I was interested & offered to collaborate with them in unravelling the mystery of this & other books. This offer he instantly declined saying that they did not require any such help. It appeared to me that they only want to know whatever is *against* the things they attack, they do not wish to hear anything that could be said on the other side. From what I have heard a large proportion of the pieces they condemn are perfectly genuine. Like everybody else, I have been taken in, & have accepted as genuine without question certain pieces, which are now believed to be spurious. But I really cannot be blamed for having done so, as everybody else is in the same boat. My own private opinion is that the Browning Sonnets is not geniune.[11] The question is where did Mr. Forman[12] obtain the "Remainder" from. I am here at Hastings slowly recovering from a long & serious illness. I cannot get about without a nurse, & am still unable to use my hand for writing. I will do my best to dictate a short article for you as soon as I have read the book. Again thanking you for the kind feeling expressed in your letter

> Believe me to be
> Yours very sincerely
> Thos. J. Wise
> P.P.   L. Wise

Pray convey my warmest regards to our good friend Mr Swann.

[July 3.]   Heartman to Wise

Carbon typescript of a cablegram, undated, but probably sent the day after the *Enquiry* was published.

CARTER POLLARD BOOK NOW BEFORE ME   STOP
NECESSITY OF DEFINITIVE STATEMENT ON YOUR PART
SEEMS IMPERATIVE   STOP   AMERICAN BOOK COLLECTOR
PROPER PLACE SINCE EDITORS SYMPATHIES ARE WITH
YOU   STOP   WILL HOLD NEXT ISSUE UNTIL END OF JULY
HEARTMAN

July 4.   Wise to Heartman

A deferred cable dispatched 1:10 p.m. this date, received
10:35 a.m. the following day.

BOOK DISGRACEFUL   STATEMENT REGARDING MY
HOLDING STOCKS OF PAMPHLETS ABSOLUTELY UNTRUE
WISE

July 19.   Wise to Heartman

Dear Mr Heartman,

I am sending you herewith a short article for your magazine as promised: I trust it will serve your purpose. I should
have liked to have written more fully, but I am still very
weak, & this heat wave reduced what little strength I have
to vanishing point & I am also swamped with correspondence.[13] I have even not yet had time to really read the
book, *critically*, but I am by no means satisfied that their
dates both regarding types & paper are correct. Any printer
could have the three distinctive letters reproduced without
any difficulty.[14] As for paper, drastic changes are not made
in a single year. In any branch of manufacture a new material takes several years to fight its way to the front. Also
the authors confine themselves to paper made in England!
they discard the fact, perhaps do not know it, that paper
made abroad from Esparto was freely imported into this
country from 1853 onwards.[15]

                    With kind regards,
                    Sincerely yours
                    Thos. J. Wise
                    P.P.   L. Wise

P.S. I hope my cablegram reached you safely.

14

The statement extends to twelve typescript pages, all revised in various ways. At least six states may be postulated:

(1) Original manuscript, dependent upon Wise, but probably written out by Frederick Page.[16]

(2) First typescript, further revised by Page, and with the connivance of Wise: still retained here in pages 4, 6-12. Text in this state may be estimated at 3170 words (12 pages $\times$ 24 lines $\times$ 11 words to a line).

(3) New typescript of four other pages, each estimated to have text reduced as follows:

	Lines		Words	Total words
Page	present	deleted	omitted	remaining
1	14	10	110	2608
2	5	19	209	
3	16	8	88	
5	9	15	165	

These deletions, it will be observed, effectively remove—perhaps again at the prompting of Page—everything which might tend to incriminate Wise. They were made at this stage, I believe, since page 3, here illustrated, is later subject to other kinds of revision.

(4) Correction of typescript readings. Manuscript and other insertions are designated by pointed brackets,[17] the first prefixed with a superscript letter indicating the kind and probable order of marks, viz:

[a]<Pencil   [b]<ink over pencil   [c]<ink

The same letters identify minor deletions, each of which, as in the original, is lined out. Alternation of pointing, in any form, is ignored.

Page 3 exhibits all these varieties of correction, as well as others listed below. At this stage Wise's hand may certainly be identified only in certain trivial inked revisions, specifically *in all probability* and *might have been* on this page, and the several alterations later in the paragraph following a quotation from the 1918 bibliography.

(5) Text augmented by two extensive annexes, both typed and here distinguished as $^d<$. Where attached these add to page 3: 115 words, page 10: 120 words. Full text now 2843 words. The additions—perhaps again at the direction of others—are designed, in the first instance, to arouse our sympathy for dear old Wise, now completely baffled by the advent of scientific bibliography and, in the second, to enforce a weak case of provenance. Both extensions occur at this stage, I suspect, because of the technique next described.

(6) Annexes linked to text and further corrected in pencil. Again as in fourth state these are marked $^a<$, since there is no way to discriminate between the two orders. Some penciling obviously was done at the earlier time, as a few of the marks are overlaid with ink; and some as obviously occur in this last state, where no ink appears. Wise's pencilling may be recognized only in the second annex $^a<$Furthermore. . . . Brantwood.$>$

As finally contrived this tortured document manages to say nothing of consequence, nothing beyond the argument advanced several times in the London *Times Literary Supplement*. Many things unsaid, or misrepresented, are duly reported in notes, as facts in the case may demand.

[July 19.]   *Certain Nineteenth Century Pamphlets*
A Personal Statement

'An Enquiry into the nature of Certain Nineteenth Century Pamphlets' by John Carter and Graham Pollard has been widely and deservedly reviewed as a most interesting detective story. Naturally it has a more painful interest for me, for the effect of the book will be to make the reader say, 'Either Mr. T. J. Wise is a forger of first and pre-first editions, or is the dupe of such a forger.' And unless the reader is as judicial as the two authors he will decide the question for himself, actuated either by his feeling for me (whether friendly or unfriendly) or by his predeliction for sensational scandal. But he cannot determine the truth, any more than the two authors can. (For the sake of brevity I shall throughout this article refer to them as "the authors"). [*10 lines deleted*]

[*Page 2*] If anyone will accept my word, here it is: I did not forge nor procure to be forged the pamphlets in question, nor any other pamphlets, nor anything, in all my life; nor have I put into circulation anything which I knew or suspected to be a forgery.[18] [*19 lines deleted*]

[*Page 3*] I cannot resist the authors' arguments from paper, type, and text, that the pamphlets they condemn as forgeries ᶜ<in all probability> are forgeries.

ᵈ<Only quite recently has it been possible to ascertain the validity of Pictures, Books, and MSS by scientific methods. But as time goes on scientists alter their opinions. This may occur in regard to the materials composing paper, and the time may arrive when some at least of these pamphlets, now for a while claimed to be frauds, will be regarded as honest books. I am an old man with ᵃ<the> crematorium facing me. Carter and Pollard are young men with long and no doubt useful lives before them, in which I wish them every success. They will assuredly live to see the day when the work of the analyst and the microscopist will be unimpeachable.>

If any single one of their arguments ought not to carry conviction to an acute and candid mind, I may trust that some one not so convinced will print a letter to say so. In the meantime I am forced to conclude that I ᶜ<in common with all my contemporaries> have been duped. The authors think that I must know or suspect who the forger was. I do not know, but in an interview reported in the *Daily Herald* of June 30 (before I had seen or read the book) I suggested that the forger ᵃ<of some of the earlier pieces> ᶜwas ᶜ<might have been> Richard Herne Shepherd.[19] The authors will not have him to be the forger. I shall not direct suspicion to anyone else, but will now ᵇ<at-

~~tempt to fulfil my promise to Mr. Pollard[20] and to~~> say when and how the 'stocks' of the pamphlets came into my hands and passed through them to Mr. Gorfin.[21] [*8 lines deleted*]

[*Page 4*] All the 'stocks' that I disposed of to Mr. Gorfin in 1910 and 1912 came to me in 1910 and 1912[22] from H. Buxton Forman, and I acted only as the intermediary and friend of both parties. The authors ask how I could in 1894 speak of *Gold Hair* (1864) as 'of the greatest rarity' and *Geist's Grave* (1881) as 'a rarity', whereas in 1910 I had 19 and 43 copies respectively, to sell to Mr. Gorfin. In 1894, sixteen years before they passed through my hands, I did not know of these stocks. Nor have I ^c<since 1910> in any catalogue of mine, ^c<~~since 1910~~> or any bibliography, spoken of them as rare. I have done no more than catalogue my own copies, and I have not catalogued anything that I knew or suspected to be a forgery, without stigmatizing it as ~~^csuspicious or fraudulent~~ ^c<fraudulent or suspicious>.

So much for the stocks of pamphlets sold to Mr. Gorfin in 1910 and 1912. Single or duplicate copies in my possession before that date came to me by the way or purchase or exchange or presentation.

The authors think it very curious (not to say suspicious) that men with whom I was then connected in business should have been selling copies of some of these pamphlets to the British Museum in 1888 and 1890 and that from 1890 onwards I should have been presenting copies to the British Museum ^a<(I have given more than 300 books and pamphlets to the British Museum alone)> and to university libraries. This must suggest that I with the help of my business friends was cunningly 'planting' forgeries [*page 5*] on the learned world. But if the reader will disentangle the facts that the authors present to him, he will realize, I think with some surprise, that Mr. Schlengemann sold two pamphlets, and no more, to the British Museum, both of them in 1888; that Mr. O. P. Rubeck sold four pamphlets, and no more, to the British Museum, all of them in 1890,[23] and beyond this only one pamphlet, to Messrs B. F. Stevens and Brown, in 1892. My associates in business were business-men, and rare books are marketable commodities. [*15 lines deleted*]

[*Page 6*] Now, once more for 'Sonnets by E. B. B. 1847'.[24]

Before the appearance of Messrs Carter and Pollard's book I had come to believe that I acquired this ᵈ<'1847'> book in 1886. But it is demonstrable that the forgery was put into circulation ᵈ~~before~~ during the last few months of 1893, neither earlier nor later, demonstrable in this way, that it is mentioned in Slater's *Early Editions* which was published about 20 January 1894, and that it is *not* mentioned in *A Catalogue of a Portion of the Library of Edmund Gosse*, issued to subscribers in November 1893. Gosse's preface to this book makes it clear that by "portion" was meant "selection",—he had selected the most interesting of his books to catalogue. It is all but certain that if he had possessed *Sonnets 1847* he would have included that in his Catalogue, especially as ᵈ<the> only two EBB items are *The Seraphim and Other Poems*, 1838, and the *Poems, New Edition*, 1850. A note to this second item says that it was the first edition in which the *Sonnets from the Portuguese* appeared. Gosse would not have stressed this if he had then been in possession of an earlier separate printing.

Messrs Carter and Pollard are ᶜ~~naturally~~ sarcastic at my expense that I should seem to confuse the classic *Sonnets* ᵃ~~from the Portugese~~ with *My Sonnets* privately printed ᵃ<in exactly the same shape, size and form> by a very minor poet.[25] Actually of course I was confusing the circumstances in which I acquired these two very different books.

in all

might
have
been

of som
the eal

[*Page 7*] I must go through my printed references to the '1847' book in date-order, to show the growth of a mistake. The dates are 1905, 1918, 1922 and 1929.

In my Catalogue of 1905 I said that my copy

'was formerly in the possession of Dr. W. C. Bennett. It was given to him by Mary Russell Mitford, to whom had been entrusted by the Authoress the task of seeing the book through the press.'

In 1918, in my Bibliography of *Elizabeth Barrett Browning* I said that

'In 1866 Dr. W. C. Bennett, who had been Miss Mitford's intimate friend, and who possessed a considerable quantity of her letters and other papers, disposed of some ten or twelve copies of the *Sonnets* which he had received from her hands.'

and I said that one of these copies, with a MS sonnet inserted, I purchased from Dr. Bennett.

In 1922 I was ᵇreprinting my ᵇ<full> Catalogue, arranged differently from ᵇ<that of> 1905 and ʰincluding later acquisitions, but/ my paragraph about the *Sonnets* simply repeats the Catalogue of 1905.

I want the reader to notice that in 1905 I (correctly) did not assert a direct purchase from Dr. Bennett. I mentioned his name only to show the pedigree (as I have up till now believed it) of my copy.

By 1918, thirteen years later, and twenty-five years after my acquisition of the book, I had slipped into regarding an indirect acquisition from Dr. Bennett as a direct purchase from him.

[*Page 8*] Eleven years later, in 1929, forty-three years after my visit to Dr. Bennett and 36 years after my acquisition of the book, I allowed myself to be garrulous about that visit. The visit was historical; the subjects of our conversation had been Miss Mitford and the Brownings; my acquisition of the '1847' book is a fact, though seven years later than the visit; the story of Dr. Bennett's association with the book I firmly believed. I had (in 1929) for at least eleven years been in the habit of thinking of the book as acquired directly from him instead of indirectly. I had come away from him in a glow of good feeling, bringing with me a book he had given me with an author's modest pride. Is it so incredible that I should connect my acquisition of the '1847' book in 1893 with that visit of 1886? The fixing of the date of the 'discovery' of the forged book as 1893 shows that our conversation could not have touched on that book. If it could have done [a]<so> he must have exploded the lie that had been so cunningly invented. I do not ask the reader to judge me charitably: I ask him to consider dispassionately this reconstruction of the growth of a delusion.

The authors make much of a supposed anonymous informant of Gosse in 1881. It seems not to have occurred to them that when Gosse in 1894 (and 1896) wrote that 'Mr. Browning, eight years before his death, made a statement to a friend', he meant that Browning made this statement to Gosse himself, and in their 'Stop Press', although they quote from my letter to the [*page 9*] *Times Literary Supplement* of May 24, 1934, they do not take any notice of my interpretation. And yet it is the natural one. 'Eight years before Browning's death' takes us back to 1881: in that year Browning was telling Gosse and partly dictating to Gosse the story of his life, and this story up to and not beyond Browning's marriage Gosse printed in the *Century Magazine*, December 1881. Gosse stopped at the marriage, and said nothing of the *Sonnets*, because Browning wished him to stop there for the time being. It is unnatural to suppose that the 'statement to a friend' in 1881, to be disclosed after Browning's death, and which was so disclosed by Gosse, was not a statement to Gosse himself. If we were to take Gosse *au pied de la lettre* it would mean that Browning told him of the '1847' book in 1881, which we now know to ~~be~~ [a]<have been> impossible. The existence of the book in 1894 and Gosse's recent acquisition of a copy[26] distorted his memory of what Browning had told him, and incidentally made him ascribe to Pisa 1847 what belonged to Bagni di Lucca 1849. The authors (I fancy) are so insistent on a supposed anonymous informant of Gosse because he would be so useful to the actual forger. I repeat emphatically that no one reading Gosse's article on 1894 (reprinted in *Critical Kitcats* 1896) in connexion with his article of 1881 (reprinted in his *Robert Browning: Personalia*, 1890) will find it unnatural to suppose that the unnamed friend was Gosse himself.

[*Page 10*] I have two more pamphlets to discuss at some length, and I shall then consider that I have made all the reply necessary to defend my own honour.[27] The first of those pamphlets is *Sir Galahad*, '1858'. I asserted the authenticity of the pamphlet in 1894, and Messrs Carter and Pollard think I should have ceased to do so after Robert Proctor had challenged its authenticity in 1898. Proctor's instinct was right: the book is now 'proved' (by the paper test) to be a fraud, but Proctor did not know of the paper test any more than I did, and his arguments were not good ones: 'for all Morris's other literary ventures at this period (1859) he employed the Chiswick Press': he had no other literary ventures at this period than *The Oxford and Cambridge Magazine* and *The Defence of Guenevere*, and it was not he but his publishers, Messrs Bell and Daldy, who employed the Chiswick Press. 'Neither Mr. Morris's family nor any of his intimate friends had ever seen or heard of the tract' before 1897; but H. Buxton Forman had one copy inscribed ᵇfor ᵇ<to> him by Morris himself, and I had another inscribed 'Ford Madox Brown from his friend William Morris'. To me these seemed good enough to establish the authenticity of the pamphlet.

In like manner I accepted George Allen's inscription on the copy of *Leoni*,[28] and Alexander Strahan's inscriptions on *The Last Tournament*, 1871, and '*A Welcome to Marie*

Alexandrovna', 1874.[29] as guarantees of their genuineness.

[d]<Furthermore I may say that proofs, both in galleys and pages, of my bibliographies of [a]<Ruskin>, Tennyson, and Swinburne were sent to [a]<Ruskin>, Hallam Tennyson and Swinburne respectively, and were read and approved by them, and [a]<none> of them questioned the pamphlets that are now objected to.

Ruskin was very pleased with the Bibliography of himself, and on its completion [a]<I was> invited ~~me~~ to Brantwood. The authors (p. 114) say that although the parts of the bibliography from September, 1889 onwards were duly sent to Ruskin he could not have examined them with any critical attention, bceause from 1885 onwards he had only intermittent intervals of lucidity during which he was able to work. I can assure them that I found him quite lucid [a]~~in 18~~ [a]<when I visited Brantwood.>>

And now I come to the most difficult problem of all,[30] although Messrs Carter and Pollard do not stress it as such: *Some College Memories*, 1886. This purports to be a private printing, [*page 11*] between the appearance of the essay in *The New Amphion*, Edinburgh, November, 1886, and its inclusion in *Memories and Portraits* 1887. Its authenticity was challenged by Messrs Constable in two letters to *The Athenaeum*, 8 and 22 January, 1898. To the first letter there was appended an editorial note, supporting the authenticity on the authority of 'a bibliographer of note' who had 'seen one copy of the grey pamphlet bearing an inscription of some length in Stevenson's handwriting'. Messrs Constable's second letter is dated the 11 January 1898 but did not appear in the issue of the 15th but for some reason was held over till the 22nd. A letter from me dated 31 January (1 am particular in mentioning all these dates because they show that the Editor and I were taking time to verify our assertions) appeared in the issue of 5 February and in it I said that the pamphlet was printed in Edinburgh at Christmas 1886, that it was authorised by Stevenson, and seen through the press by Mr. W. H. Hepworth, 'one of Stevenson's most valued friends and correspondents'. Three weeks later, in the *Athenaeum*, 26 February, appeared a satirical letter from the bookseller, Mr. Frank T. Sabin, in which the ghost of R.L.S. is made to say that it 'must remain an undiscoverable secret' why he employed an anonymous printer, why he did not ask Messrs Constable's permission, why he did not borrow their block of the vignette portrait on the title page instead of having a ~~very inferior copy~~ [a]<reproduction> made, and why he informed none of his Edinburgh friends.

[*Page 12*] To these supposed unanswerable queries, Messrs Carter and Pollard add the difficulty that Mr. W. H. Hepworth, 'one of Stevenson's most valued friends and correspondents', does not appear in Stevenson's [a]<published> correspondence, nor can he be traced after 1896. [a]<The correspondence may quite well exist and may some day appear.> In 1905 I spoke of him as 'the late Mr. W. H. Hepworth', but his will is not to be found at Somerset House between the years 1886 and 1910; nor have some enquiries which a friend is making for me yet borne fruit. Nevertheless I firmly believe in this Mr. W. H. Hepworth [a]<(see my introduction to *The Bibliography of Ruskin*)> whose name I had from my friend J. P. Smart, who collaborated with me in *The Bibliography of Ruskin*, but I myself had seen the grey pamphlet with the inscription of some length in Stevenson's handwriting. And there I must leave the matter for the present.

[c]<Thomas J. Wise>

July 19-22.   Wise to Heartman

The very day Wise's statement was posted his friend Frederick Page conferred with Messrs Carter and Pollard. Page, an official with the Oxford University Press, came to the meeting not without some confidence that he could extract information useful to Wise. He left it, an hour later, so disturbed that he could barely compose his thoughts. Yet all that passed had to be set out, formally, so that there would be no misunderstanding on either side. As an intermediary the task was his, and he soon performed it in a long and carefully worded letter. That communication, the Enquirers insisted, was still not so precise as the situation required.[31] Nonetheless, the early and only recorded version[32] indicates, for one side, that Page himself had drawn up the letter Wise printed in the *Times Literary Supplement* 24 May and, further, that he had materially assisted in the preparation of the statement. To the other side it now was evident that, if the statement, like the letter, shifted any blame upon Harry Buxton Forman, without sufficient documentation, the Enquirers were ready to divulge other evidence of Wise's complicity. As the statement of the 19th did exactly that, Page strongly urged Wise to recall it.

Whether Wise was warned by letter, or by telephone, the message was soon received, and he immediately reacted in the cable which follows. This is a night letter, received by Heartman's nearest telegraph office, Metuchen, N.J. 9:04 a.m. on 22 July.

I HAVE DECIDED THAT I CANNOT ALLOW MY ARTICLE TO BE PRINTED   PLEASE RETURN IT IMMEDIATELY   I AM LETTING CARTER AND POLLARD KNOW THAT I HAVE WITHDRAWN THE ARTICLE   WILL WRITE

WISE

July 30.   Heartman to Wise

Perhaps some eight days after he had the cable Heartman received, by sea-mail, the statement. This curious performance, he realized, was too valuable to be returned, and yet, as Wise and others had demanded, something must be sent back. Though the following letter gives no hint of Heartman's decision, a filed carbon provides a clue. Wise probably got the original of this fair copy and, in his distracted state, was unable to tell the difference or, if he did, to protest the switch. Or possibly, Heartman may have declared, in a dispatch unpreserved, that the original typescript had been immediately destroyed upon preparation of this fair copy.[33]

Dear Mr. Wise:

I am very sorry that you will not let me print your paper which I think is an excellent defense. However, it is up to you what you want to do. Everybody feels very bad about the matter here. I have tried hard to take your side in at least pointing out circumstances which should exonerate you but I cannot do anything if you do not help me. After all, there is a powerful clique here working against you.[34] Of course, if there are circumstances which put a different aspect on the matter I shall feel very sorry.

I am awaiting your letter which perhaps will explain matters. In the meantime the magazine will go to press today without any word from you and in your defense.

Sincerely yours,
Charles F. Heartman

July 31.   Wise to Heartman

This letter crossed the one written by Heartman the day before. Since Wise had failed to measure up to his expectations the disappointed publisher saw no reason to answer this or the two letters following.

Dear Mr Heartman,

Shortly after I had posted the hastily written article I had put together for you, I completed reading the book, & at once saw that the article in its present state was most unsuitable. I therefore cabled you to withdraw it from press, & to return the article to me, which of course you will have done. That article was simply a repitition [*sic*] in other words of my letters to the Times Literary Supplement. What I must do is to make a careful study of the contents of the book, & write a thoughtful Review of it. When this is ready I will, of course communicate with you. Everyone knew that I was sending you an article, & the authors would take this as meaning an *attack*. I therefore let them know that I had withdrawn it.

Believe me to be
Always sincerely yours
Thos. J. Wise
P.P. L. Wise

P.S. Of course the foregoing is private and confidential, and not for publication, as also were my two cablegrams to you.

August 19.   Wise to Heartman

Private and *confidential*
Dear Mr Heartman,

I received the new number of the American Book Collector, & thank you for sending it. I have read the article & entirely approve of it. Of all the notices in America that I have seen yours is almost the only one written fairly & without prejudice. In particular I have to thank you for your expression of Confidence on page 272,[35] but in the last line of that paragraph should be several *hundred*, not *thousand* pounds. May I draw your attention to some remarks made in Mitchell Kennerley's letter. He says "Mr. Forman was not a bookseller, whereas Mr Wise has been a busy book seller since the days of his youth." Did Mr Kennerley stand by the side of Mr Forman, & by my side, for a period of 50 years! As to temporary estrangement over an offer to purchase two Shelley books, the suggestion is absurd!
I have already written to you about my intention with

regard to the future. When the proper time arrives I shall of course communicate with you.

Very Sincerely Yours
Thos. J. Wise
P.P. L. Wise

January 28, 1935.   Wise to Heartman

Confidential

Dear Mr Heartman,

Thanks for your note regarding the 1935 subscription to The A.B.C. Enclosed is cheque 13/- to cover it.

I have this morning received a letter from a friend in New York to say that in the recent Eckel Sale a copy of Stevenson's "Story of a Lie" sold for $130.00. So evidently *some* people in America hold the same opinion that most folk here do,—namely that—the little book is perfectly genuine in spite of what Messrs Carter & Pd say. I myself have always believed that the little batch discovered by Colonel Prideaux and purchased by Mr. Forman were "right" in every way.[36]

Sincerely yours,
[s] Thos. J. Wise

2. Heartman and His Readers

July 3-10, 1934.   The Overture

Immediately upon issue of the *Enquiry*, and for seven days thereafter, Heartman's secretary worked round the clock typing individual letters to every important subscriber of his *American Book Collector*. As the stationery ran out another supply, with a different letterhead, was hastily ordered.[37] Soon all his selected readers, many of them only halfway through the book, had an unusual request.

[Name of correspondent]
THE AMERICAN BOOK COLLECTOR in its next issue will have an extended account of the sensational exposure made by Messrs. Carter and Pollard. We will try very hard to get a statement from Mr. Wise. It is unfortunate this affair happened and will undoubtedly be an additional burden to be carried both by rare book dealers and collectors.

We would like to give the most extended account of this affair going into it from every angle in order that we may never have to come back to it. We certainly would be of great service to the book collecting world if we could assemble as many opinions as possible of well known collectors and the editor is asking you to write us a letter within the next few weeks expressing your reaction to this whole affair. These letters will not be edited.

You will be fully at liberty to say what you please but we do feel that a consensus of opinion may have some element of reassurance for the harassed collector. There is no limit to the length of the letter and we will not object to any irrelevant matters which might be brought into the situation. Considering your interest in collecting we hope that this request will not be in vain.

> Very truly yours,
> THE AMERICAN BOOK COLLECTOR
> [s] Charles F. Heartman
> Editor

July 8-23.   The Response

For the most part Heartman's new campaign, represented in yet another file, met with dead silence. Various readers who did reply were noncommittal or, while acknowledging the necessity of some comment, yet put off the evil day. Typical remarks follow.

Walter M. Hill:[38] "I prefer to refrain from saying or writing anything about it. . . . I have been wishing for some time I was out of the business."

Owen D. Young: "I have not time enough at my disposal to look into the matter."

M. L. Parrish: "Mr. Wise has already made his statement in 'The Times'. I have no comment to make."

W. T. H. Howe: "I shall not be able to accede to your request . . . at the present time."

Barton Currie: "I hope to be able to get off my letter to you about the middle of next week." Even this definite promise, however, was unfulfilled.

A sharp response from Gertrude Hills[39] was, perhaps, too strongly worded for Heartman to print. It concludes: "Indeed if all dishonest, half-informed, or half-baked rare book 'esparto' dealers, bibliographers, cataloguers & article writers cd be cleaned out, by its returned health the book business wd again come into its own." Another from Miss Ratchford, rare-book librarian at Texas, expresses her resentment at the "sensational journalism" attending the publication. This too Heartman could not print, since she forbade it.

July 24-30   The Publication

Out of all this activity, then, the net result was three letters fit for issue in Heartman's August-September number. With his own review of the *Enquiry* (pp. 233-41) already composed, Heartman on July 24 (as he says in print) introduced these under the title "The Greatest Rare Book Sensation" (pp. 241-44). Fortunately of the three the longest and best, and the one Wise found most objectionable (see above, p. 28–29), was received just that day. This, from Mitchell Kennerley, warmly commends the Enquirers and denounces the forger, of whose identity he had no doubt. The second, from one Henry M. Partridge, provides a welcome diversion by laying all charges against Mark Twain, an author he had previously accused of writing *Alice in Wonderland* and much of Hawthorne. The third, from

31

Gabriel Wells, simply pines for better days, a wish repeated verbatim in the pamphlet he later prepared. With these three letters on record, and the all-important statement withdrawn, Heartman on July 30th, as he then informed Wise (p. 27 above), went to press.

ca. September 15.   The Aftermath
When the October issue was readied for the printer, Heartman regretfully closed the correspondence on the *Enquiry* (p. 309) pending definite news. Two pages later he opened it again to announce that, in view of "written and properly signed statements,"[40] he was convinced that Messrs Carter and Pollard had positive proof of Wise's guilt.

From this time forward Heartman, his campaigns all at an end, exerted himself only once, this in a letter to Wells, whose several activities were now just under way. Accordingly, though it is in the present *Collector* file, the letter is deferred until it may properly serve as a conclusion to all that Wells now attempts.

3. Wells and Wise
September 19.

In his own copy of *The Carter-Pollard Disclosures* Gabriel Wells filed the carbon of a typescript letter he had sent to Mrs Wise, representing the endeavor which now concerns us, and two letters addressed to him, both pertaining to his later campaign. Of this earlier effort the only previous report, in Partington's biography of Wise, seemed almost beyond belief. Now that it is authenticated, however, the biography serves as the most appropriate introduction.

One day I [Wells] went to Heath Drive with the idea of making an end of the unsatisfactory position. Tom was very excited. He was willing to do anything. And I even drew up a statement, a confession, for him to sign, of his part in the business, and of his willingness to make recompense for any direct loss sustained through him. But the final decision was not to touch it—that it was best left alone.

Myself: But was Wise willing to sign this document?
Gabriel Wells: Oh, yes!
Myself: You are certain he understood it was a confession?
Gabriel Wells: Certain! But it was thought best to leave it alone; and there I left it.

Subsequently I sent Gabriel Wells a copy of the above note of our conversation, asking if he had any objection to my using it. At an interview which he requested, to discuss the proposal, he said that the only objection he had was the use of the word 'confession', and that all else was accurate. He averred that there had been no confession, and that I must have misunderstood him. But my note was written within an hour of the conversation. While I print it as an accurate record of what was said, it is only fair to give equal prominence to his subsequent objection to the one word.[41]

September 20.   Wells to Mrs. Wise

The day after his visit to Heath Drive, Wells took counsel with two prominent booksellers and then drafted the following letter. The final copy sent to Mrs. Wise presumably did not contain the reference here deleted.

My dear Mrs. Wise,
    After a most careful and thorough consideration of the case, and having had a long ~~conference with the Maggs~~ <discussion of the matter with two judicious and well informed gentlemen> this morning, I have come to the definite conclusion that the wisest course in the circumstances is to maintain a dignified silence. He has so many staunch friends of the highest caliber, who have implicit faith in his integrity, that he can well afford to let the affair

rest on that. Besides, he is not in a condition to conduct a controversy, which any statement of his is sure to evoke. Also, any remark, however discreetly done that would point the finger to others would not be taken kindly by the public generally; and might lead collectors to feel that if Buxton Forman, for example, could have done it then why hesitate to suspect without tangible evidence to the contrary a man likewise to be of fine and spotless character.

To know oneself to be innocent, and to have disinterested, loyal friends believe so, that should be sufficient.

Please destroy the draft I handed you yesterday, and by no means let him do anything further in the matter.

Possibly when I return to America I may on my own have something to say for publication shewing the honesty and sterling character of the man. After all, moral judgment must be based upon a person as a whole.

With kindest regards and best wishes to you both.

> Sincerely,
> [s] Gabriel Wells

4. *The Carter-Pollard Disclosures*

The sense of urgency which so impelled Wells, first to approach Wise with a statement (or confession?), and now to contemplate another on his own account, doubtless arose from correspondence printed in the *Times Literary Supplement*. After Wise had promised that, on a more careful reading of the *Enquiry*, he would have "something to say" (July 12), few readers could tolerate his continued silence. The pressure was ever increasing, as Partington makes clear, and was further intensified by Viscount Esher, who opened his letter (August 23) with a reminder:

> Book collectors throughout the world are still waiting to hear from Mr. Wise an explanation of the forgeries exposed by Mr. Carter and Mr. Pollard....

And closed it with a demand:

A considerable time has elapsed, and the collectors who have followed Mr. Wise have a right to know how they stand in the matter.

Against this the excuse of illness, offered over the signature of Mrs. Wise (August 30), was completely unacceptable.

Having withdrawn the one, Wells on reaching New York resolved upon a second statement. There some reference must be made to Esher (and so it appears, p. 10); the earlier remarks Heartman had printed would also be useful (p. 12); and several sentences in the letter to Mrs. Wise were worth repeating (p. 11). Beyond all that the tract could rest primarily on faith, hope, and charity, but certainly not on any of the pamphlets. Thus determined, Wells sought final encouragement, and was immediately rebuffed.

October 14.   Tinker to Wells

Among all American reviewers of the *Enquiry* Chauncey B. Tinker, Professor of English at Yale University, was perhaps the most erudite and, happily, the most charitable. He had mildly labeled his own survey "A Bibliographical Hoax"[42]—an interpretation G. B. Shaw was later to adopt; he was ready to accept, provisionally, the defense that large numbers of the forgeries "came into the hands of Mr. Wise as 'remainders' "; and he was, moreover, a good friend of Wells. What Wells now proposed, however, was quite impossible.

Dear Mr. Wells,

I appreciate the nobility of motive that lies behind your letter about Mr. Wise; but I do not believe that it can save him from the contempt and anger that people feel. They have a right to some sort of explanation, and if Wise is unable to make one, somebody else ought to do it for him. Otherwise he will end his life in disgrace. If a committee consisting of A. W. Pollard and Chapman[43] were to present his explanation to the public, something might be accomplished, but this silence is, as an English friend writes me, 'fatal'. It is for this reason that I ventured to criticize your letter about the subject. It seems to me to provide a poultice rather than a cure.

You must pardon my frankness; it is seldom that I disagree with you on such matters.

Yours sincerely,
[s] C. B. Tinker

October 15.   Newton to Wells

Alarmed at Wells's folly, Professor Tinker also wrote at once to A. E. Newton, a collector known and admired for his well-publicized zest for the game. Newton was even closer to Wells, and in years past to Wise, for whom he had provided an enthusiastic introduction to volume VI (1925) of the *Ashley Library*. Perhaps then, so Tinker hoped, Newton could bring additional weight to bear against this mad scheme. The reaction was immediate.

My dear Gabriel:

I was sorry not to have a word with you on Saturday, but we were delayed in reaching New York. We had a pleasant week-end with the Osgoods at Princeton, and on my desk this morning I find a letter from Tinker in which he says you are thinking of writing something in regard to Wise. I beg you not to do so unless you are prepared to swear on a bunch of bibles that you know to your own knowledge that Wise is entirely innocent of any connection, however remote, with the pamphlets in question. Every word that Wise has said in his own behalf or that has been said for him only tends to weaken his position. I tried to prevent the publication of the book[44] but I found myself unable satisfactorily to answer Carter's arguments for publishing now.

I shall certainly see you in New York before sailing.

Yours sincerely
[s] A. Edward Newton

October 20.   Heartman to Wells

Quite undeterred by the best advice, Wells rushed into print with his *Carter-Pollard Disclosures* and, after a day or two, elicited from the first campaigner a very hostile response.

Dear Mr. Wells:

I have postponed writing you this letter but I have to get it off my chest. After having read your pamphlet twice I feel more sorry than ever that you published it. I have been asked by a number of persons to rip hell out of it. Some of them are probably the same persons who praised the booklet to your face. Some day you will believe that I am sincere with you and try to see things as they are to your interest.

The pamphlet is one of those things where the counsel for defence makes what he thinks is an able case but which the prosecuting attorney could tear to pieces. On the first page you accuse the authors of not being strictly objective but having indulged in personalities. But isn't your pamphlet after all also an indulgence in personalities? Somewhere you say that those who were unsparing in their pronouncements were often persons who cannot be considered irreproachable in their own conduct. This is a very unfortunate sentence. You mean to imply that Michael Sadleir, Lord Esher, Leonard Mackall,[45] just to mention a few, are criticisable as far as their conduct is concerned? This sentence will go very bitter against you. In fact, if anybody in England wanted to, they might go after you for libel. It does not matter that you do not mention names as I have found out to my own sorrow. In England anybody who got mixed up with the matter could consider your lines as libelous to him and take action. Probably nobody will do this but it certainly will bring about resentment.

There is positive evidence that for twenty years well known names have considered the "Sonnets" and some of the other items as fakes.[46] They have also told Mr. Wise so. That this never went into print was done out of regard for a number of nice people who were mixed up in the distribution of some of these pamphlets and they also hoped that Mr. Wise would find a way of repudiating those things. Nothing has created more comment than your remarks about Mr. Wise never once having offered a book for sale to you when there are dozens of persons to whom he has constantly offered books, quite often in gushing terms beneath the dignity of any seller. That he actually sold, in fact made bookselling his secondary hobby, is too well known even to be discussed. Everybody thinks you had very ulterior motives in saying what you did.

When you say Mr. Wise might have drawn support in the compilation of the catalogue from the fact that the pamphlets in question were all finding a recognized and long established place in the great libraries you must know that this is not tentative. He was the only one who built up a background and cataloguers who wanted to go against quotations from Wise's bibliographies were told to shut up. It certainly sounds amazing that you consider anyone who now wants the truth to be a slanderer. You say Mr. Wise could not draw reliably on his memory nor was there strength enough to deal with the insinuations. I think this is terrible. Nobody knows better than I that one's memory is not to be trusted and even what at one time was an incident of great importance in ones life begins as years go by to fade into something not to be distinctly remembered but certainly if one can trace to one source the selling of two thousand fakes which was done over a period of years, memory has nothing to do with it. One knows quite well all about it.

There is no need to go further into this. As far as my magazine is concerned I shall refer to your pamphlet only in a few lines although it could be made a base of a sensational article.[47] It is not loyalty to you which makes me suppress my own feeling and the statements of others in this matter although I suppose that has a little to do with it. I am refraining from going into it mainly because I promised myself to keep quiet. But I must emphasize again that I do feel sorry that this pamphlet was published. You have established quite a literary standing and this apology for Mr. Wise which is a very weak plea will not add to your reputation as a sound writer. The worse on this affair, of course, is that it will be definitely proven that your plea was a misplaced charitable act which should not have gone out in print.

I shall see you sometime this week and we can talk about it some more.

Sincerely yours,
[s] Charles F. Heartman

So end these communications, all creating a great disturbance, but none to any good effect. The only "convincing answer," as Tinker had said in his review, would necessarily "fill a book as long and as admirably documented" as the *Enquiry* itself. That book we shall never see. The new volume by the Enquirers, however, will meet every other expectation.

Postscript on *The Story of a Lie*

To substantiate the assertion (p. 29, n. 36) that it was Wise who first "authenticated" this Stevenson forgery, it is necessary, first of all, to reexamine the earliest printings of 1901-1905 of the *Ashley Library* catalogue. Altogether, there appear to be at least seven issues: [1] one perhaps correctly designated, as it is called, a specimen, [2] another trial "complete" for its period, [3-5] three others consisting of mixtures of finished sheets, early proofs, or later impressions, and [6-7] two final issues. Only in [2-7] is there an entry for *The Story*, and there it invariably appears, in identical setting, as the initial item on page 139 (S2^r). Except for [2] all copies are now represented at Texas.

[1] *(Specimen) March.* 1901. So described at head of front wrapper. Issue of 72 pp., none including the entry in question. Wove paper, the John Johnson-John Carter copy (lot 13 in the Pariser sale).

[2] 1901. Title of same setting as [1], collation A-S^4, entries in three alphabetical sequences, the last ending p. 144 with three Waller items. Throughout on Whatman paper dated 1900. Though apparently not extant now in separate form, this would seem to have been issued originally in 1901.

[3] 1901. Issue [2], as just described, to which has been added another section collating T-II^4 and representing a fourth alphabetical sequence together with miscellaneous items, the last group ending p. 245 with three Dryden entries. Thin wove paper. This later section, severely weather-beaten and stained on first and last leaves, must have lain exposed and apart for at least four years, as it is of the *corrected* state of the corresponding sheets next described. The Pariser copy (lot 14).

[4] 1901. Another issue divided as in [3], and thus also, perhaps, once existing originally in several variants. The 1901 title first part is followed by a 12-leaf proof insert, first leaf with title dated 1905. Remainder of this section, through gathering S, on wove paper. Second section, now collating T-II^4 χ^4 ($-\chi 4$) KK^4, consists usually of thinner wove proof sheets, gatherings stamped by Richard Clay &

Sons 11 Feb. 1904–8 Mar. 1905; final text page 262 (KK3^v) concludes a Gay entry and cites another for Brome, this limited to 9 lines; recto of last leaf illustrates the Ashley device. MS corrections on proofs are generally incorporated in text second section of issue [3]. The Pariser copy (lot 15).

[5] 1905. A completely integrated book excepting an insert of two smaller proof leaves A2–3, collation now beginning π^2[A]–[D]^{4}E– and concluding without the previously inserted gathering. Mixture of Whatman 1904 and wove paper. On page 262 the Brome entry is now extended to 15 lines, followed as in [4] by the Ashley device. The Aitken copy, with his annotations.

[6] 1905. Integrated, collation now beginning $^1\pi^2$ $^2\pi^4$ $^3\pi^4$ [A] B–, other points as in [5]. Wove paper throughout, sixe 12 x 9½″, a.e.g., Inscribed by Wise to Wrenn.

[7] 1905. Integrated, all points as in [6]. Whatman 1904 paper throughout, sixe 12 x 9⅝″, t.e.g. Apparently of this issue Texas has also a smaller copy (10½ x 8½″), with watermark trimmed, and bearing several notations in the hand of Wise and others.

The crux of this long account is, that if we accept [2] as separately prepared at the date assigned, then Wise two years before the publication of W. F. Prideaux's bibliography had already proclaimed and continued to reiterate that the forged *Story of a Lie* was intended "for publication in 1882, but was withdrawn at the last moment, and the entire impression destroyed. Very few sets of the sheets were preserved." Further hints may be found in Wise's letters to Prideaux (29 of them 1901–1908 deposited at Texas), one of which, November 2, 1901, expresses his surprise that the Colonel was well along with a Stevenson bibliography. Wise's own endeavor, he then confesses, was being prepared for *The Bookman*, "but I suppose all that can quickly drop!" Several times thereafter Prideaux was invited to visit the Wises, and on one of these occasions doubtless was given a preliminary catalogue, the entries pertaining to Stevenson, or even a copy of *The Story* itself. In any event, to make sure that Prideaux had all the stories straight, Wise on January 6, 1903, asked if he might have a "peep at your R.L.S. proofs." All was well, apparently, for Prideaux at times simply paraphrased Wise and never once dared contradict him.

Notes

1. John Carter and Graham Pollard, *An Enquiry into the Nature of Certain Nineteenth Century Pamphlets*, London and New York, 1934. An augmented edition, in two volumes, is due for publication by the University of Chicago Press.

2. Another assortment of memorabilia, including several letters, and notes by the compiler, Falconer Madan, is at the Bodleian Library, shelfmark 258492.d.7. Hereafter this will be identified as "Bodleian file."

3. The six known to the editor: the Brownings, Eliot, Kipling, Swinburne, Tennyson. The nine then unknown: Arnold, Dickens, Morris, Rossetti, Ruskin, Stevenson, Thackeray, Wordsworth, Yates.

4. Though some doubt was expressed at the time (Bodleian file) as to the severity of Wise's illness, it would appear that from June to October 1934 all correspondence was dictated to his wife Frances Lois Wise and, as will appear later, all formal statements prepared by or with the assistance of others.

5. Diligent readers of the introduction to Miss Fannie Ratchford's edition of *Letters of Thomas J. Wise to John Henry Wrenn* (New York, 1944), p. 54, will discover that she had seen the document and perhaps too hastily dismissed it as adding "nothing of information or interest to his several published statements."

6. Arthur Swann, a highly respected auctioneer, was at this time head of the American Art Association.

7. Twice mentioned in the letter. This first reference is to the son, Maurice Buxton Forman, now and for some time to come Wise's constant attendant and ready buffer against rude questions about the forgeries.

8. As Mr. Carter informs me (letter of October 9, 1967), he had often listened to Wise's discourses over a cup of tea at Elkin Mathews, and on one occasion was admonished as erroneous for reporting an earlier state of Byron's *Manfred*, which Wise himself then later trumpeted as a major variant "in the collection of my friend Oliver Chadwick-Healey." (Three issues are recognized in Wise's several accounts—*The Ashley Library*, 1922. I. 155–6; *A Byron Library*, 1928, p. 56; *A Bibliography of Byron*, 1932, I 121—but none there designated as owned by any certain person.) Also before this time Mr. Carter and Wise had corresponded on bibliographical matters. (See Sotheby Auction Catalogue, December 4–5, 1967, lot 366A. Hereafter this reference is designated Pariser sale.)

9. Mr. Pollard was then aged thirty-one.

10. Actually October 12, when Mr. Pollard asked for information as to where and when Wise had acquired numerous copies of pamphlets identified in a list then submitted to him. See Wilfred Partington, *Thomas J. Wise in the Original Cloth* (London, 1945) pp. 267–8; also *Enquiry*, p. 151.

11. An admission not previously conveyed in print. In a letter prepared by Frederick Page (see note 16 below), and printed in the *Times Literary Supplement* May 24, Wise pleads some confusion between these Sonnets of "1847" (ca. 1893) and W. C. Bennett's *Sonnets* of 1843. Later in the *TLS* for May 31, and probably again under the same aegis, he shifted responsibility for this and all other acquisitions to the elder Forman, identified in next note.

12. As against the earlier allusion (note 7), the reference now is to the father, Harry Buxton Forman (1842-1917), a friend whose complicity will be further examined very closely in the new Carter-Pollard edition (note 1). A. W. Pollard, in a letter January 16, 1935, to Madan (Bodleian file), says of Wise: "I think he is too honest to

have done it, and I also greatly doubt whether he is clever enough! He does not seem to me to have the kind of brain which could have produced [the forgeries]." It seems likely that Pollard was the anonymous but highly respected bibliographer whose opinion to the same effect dissuaded several members of the Roxburghe Club from moving to expel Wise. (After much private debate he was in December 1934 persuaded to resign on grounds of health without the issue being raised.)

13. All these excuses hardly suffice for what follows. Wise's physical incapacity cannot be assessed, but the maximum temperature in London this day was only 75°, and the correspondence could well have been deferred. All that counted now was the *Enquiry*, a work completely undermining Wise's scholarly reputation and demanding his every wakeful moment. To say—as he does in the next sentence—that he has not yet read the book *critically*, seventeen days after issue, simply indicates that he finds it unanswerable.

14. This lame explanation, probably again upon expert advice, was not advanced in formal statements. Any unusual circumstance producing bastardized type—the evidence for condemning many of the pamphlets—could hardly recur, accidentally, to produce an identical bastard elsewhere.

15. Very probably Wise had now just received proofs of an article by William Talbot (*The Bookseller*, July 11) endeavoring to prove the earlier use of esparto grass: a contention adequately refuted by the Enquirers in subsequent issues.

16. In his interview with the Enquirers on July 19 Page, an official of the Oxford University Press, admitted writing for Wise the *TLS* letter of May 24 (see note 11) and, on this latter occasion, stressed as particularly objectionable the very matters emphasized in the statement. Throughout, as Mr. Carter reassures me, the styling of the

declaration is of Page's judicious construction, one quite dissimilar to Wise's pompous idiom and syntax.

17. Necessarily, for want of evidence, the same mark is used for several words which may have been corrected initially at the time of original typing.

18. Against this sweeping disavowal only one particular need be cited, Wise's interlinear remark to Forman: "We print 'Last Tournament' in 1896, & want 'someone to think' it was printed in 1871!" *Between the Lines*, ed. Fannie E. Ratchford (Austin, 1945), plate 22b. The complicity of both Wise and Forman, as evidenced in this statement, will be more precisely assessed in the augmented edition of the *Enquiry*.

19. A clipping from the *Daily Herald* is in the Bodleian file. Shepherd (d. 1895), though known in his own time for piratical activities, could not have been involved in many of the fifty-four printings now arraigned, since his own bibliographical references, or provenance or dating, put some of them beyond his period. See *Enquiry*, p. 122.

20. The promise made October 12, 1933, when Wise was first approached. See above, Wise's June 25 letter to Heartman.

21. Herbert E. Gorfin (1878–1942), formerly an employee in the Rubeck-Wise firm of essential oils and Wise's factotum there, latterly the bookseller to whom, as the Enquirers demonstrate (pp. 371–8), Wise sold 558 copies of questionable or demonstrably fraudulent pamphlets.

22. As early as 1894, however, Wise was dispatching smaller lots to J. E. Cornish, a Manchester bookseller. See *Thomas J. Wise Centenary Studies*, ed. William B. Todd (Austin and Edinburgh, 1959), pp. 20–29.

23. As noted in the Pariser sale (lot 472) two of these at least were forgeries and, as again noted in *Wise after the Event* (ed. G. E. Haslam, Manchester, 1964, p. 69), Rubeck attempted to foist off yet another upon C. Wentworth Wass.

24. This befuddled and misleading argument about Elizabeth Barrett Browning's *Sonnets* should be assessed, in its entirety, against the account in *Centenary Studies*, pp. 57–8.

25. That is, W. C. Bennett's *My Sonnets*, 1843, a pamphlet not quite the same in "shape, size and form." Unlike the other, this is an octavo in fours, ⅛″ less in height and width, and of entirely different typography.

26. As indicated in *Centenary Studies*, pp. 59–61, there is good reason to believe that Gosse never had a copy.

27. At this point, after very extensive textual deletions, Wise has chosen, or been instructed, to refer at length to one pamphlet (the *Sonnets*), incidentally to two others. Now with only slight amendments he considers two more and casually refers to three others. All these eight doubtless represent the ones where he may best defend himself, or best avoid discovery; yet they hardly suffice, either in themselves, or against the forty-six others unmentioned, as a proper justification of his "honour."

28. Of the three pamphlets just mentioned the Enquirers doubt the authenticity of the signature in the first (p. 210), are of the opinion that the second is on an inserted leaf (p. 207), and have no record of any George Allen inscription (pp. 236–237).

29. Very probably these inscriptions were secured in 1904 when, to Wise's great surprise, Strahan was discovered to be "very much alive" and planning "to spend an evening & talk Tennyson" with him (letter January 30 to Forman, cited by Fannie E. Ratchford in *Review of Reviews* [Austin, 1946], p. 48). This elderly gentleman, then aged 74, was induced into signing not only the forgery first cited, and supposedly published by his firm, but also the second, purportedly issued by "Henry S. King & Co."

30. Among all "problems" this is actually the one most susceptible to explanation, and thus here treated at length.

31. The Carter file, to which I have been allowed access, clearly defines certain amendments, all of which were adopted by Page in his second version.

32. *Letters from Wise to Wrenn*, p. 52–3.

33. The original Wise statement is on standard size English paper 10 x 8″, the carbon of the fair typescript on American paper 11 x 8½″.

34. Apparently just another ploy in Heartman's campaign. No one then or now has any knowledge of a "powerful clique."

35. "I still believe in him. Those who think that his contradictions of incidents which happened so long ago, speak not well for him, might test their own memory in matters which happened, say, only fifteen years ago." Wise's later reference to *hundred* is his estimate of total value of books given to the British Museum.

36. No such "little batch" was ever mentioned, and the tale actually concocted, as indicated in a postscript above (p. 39–42), originated not with Prideaux but with Wise himself.

37. The first lot bears a telephone number in letterhead and was in use ca. July 3 (copy of that date addressed to Wrenn Library); the second has no number and was in use July 10 (when a letter of that date was sent to M. L. Parrish). The original typing may be further recognized in the text, which awkwardly reads, beginning of third sentence: "It is an unfortunate affair to have happened. . . ."

38. Hill was one of the main American retail distributors for the forgeries; the others here mentioned were all respected bibliophiles.

39. Mrs. Hills was employed, at least from 1939 to 1941, by E. J. Beinecke, and did much to elucidate his great Stevenson collection, now at Yale University.

40. Presumably the Gorfin affidavits, shortly to be reported by the Enquirers.

41. Partridge, *op. cit.*, pp. 290–1.

42. *The Saturday Review of Literature*, August 11, 1934, pp. 45–6.

43. Pollard had already expressed his views privately (note 12 above), but R. W. Chapman never seems to have given his opinion, though it was rumored that, for some years thereafter, he remained one of Wise's few remaining advocates.

44. Newton's intervention, in a letter of January 6, 1934, is quoted at some length in the Pariser sale, lot 370.

45. Of these three bibliophiles perhaps the least known, now, is Leonard L. Mackall, in 1933 elected second vice-president of the Bibliographical Society of America, and in 1934 recognized as the author of the longest series of reviews of the *Enquiry* and attending correspondence (*New York Herald-Tribune*, July 15, 22, 29, August 5, 19).

46. Early printed warnings against the forgeries are documented by Mr. Carter, *Centenary Studies*, p. 5, n. 1.

47. Heartman later decided to ignore this foolish act, both in his Journal and in his detailed *Bibliography* of Wells, issued 1939 in "less than two hundred copies."

500 copies of this book have been printed at the Printing Division of The University of Texas. The text is set in Waverley with Hermann Zapf's Palatino used for titling and headings. Designed by William R. Holman